Cryptocurrency

Gaining Proficiency In Its Technologies And Exploiting Investment And Trading Opportunities

(An Introductory Manual For Gaining Proficiency In Fintech And Achieving Success)

Ravinder Connor

TABLE OF CONTENT

What Is Cryptocurrency?.. 1

Selecting Your Ethereum Wallet.. 8

Investing In Stablecoins 16

Systems For Identity And Reputation 45

Using Macd Indicators 63

The Blockchain..82

Mining With Cryptocurrency 103

What Is Cryptocurrency?

A cryptocurrency, colloquially known as "crypto," functions as a means of payment for the acquisition of goods and services in online settings. Certain enterprises issue their own proprietary currencies, commonly known as tokens, which are primarily intended for the purpose of facilitating the acquisition of the company's products or services via trade.

Consider cryptocurrencies as the equivalent of chips employed in casino establishments or tokens purchased for the purpose of engaging in arcade game activities. You will engage in the substitution of tangible currency in order to acquire a specific digital currency as a means of obtaining entry to the offered service or product.

Cryptocurrency can be characterized as a decentralized digital currency.

It operates on a blockchain, a decentralized technology that is distributed across numerous computer systems responsible for managing and documenting transactions. One notable benefit of this technology lies in its robust security measures. Cryptocurrencies are safeguarded through cryptographic technology, rendering them exceedingly resistant to double-spending or counterfeiting.

A notable attribute of cryptocurrencies lies in their lack of issuance by any central authority, rendering them potentially impervious to governmental manipulation or interference in theory.

Cryptocurrencies are generated through distinct computer encryption methods that enable the establishment of a restricted quantity of monetary units, commonly known as coins. Subsequently, these currencies undergo verification to facilitate secure fund transfers.

The production method is commonly known as mining due to its theoretical resemblance to the extraction of precious metals and gold. In order to engage in the process of "cryptocurrency mining", one must undertake the task of solving a intricate algorithm or puzzle. Mining cryptocurrency is a costly endeavor; thus, it is not feasible to generate value from nothing. The integrity of these currencies is safeguarded by the principles of mathematics, rather than being reliant on any governing central bank or governmental authority.

The proliferation of cryptocurrency usage is on a constant rise, accompanied by a corresponding expansion of its real-world user base. Similar to the utilization of tangible currency, cryptocurrency permits the acquisition of various commodities encompassing physical products, event admissions, sports events, prepaid vouchers, as well as lodging reservations. Certain establishments in the food and beverage industry have begun to embrace digital currencies as a viable method of transaction. Moreover, certain non-governmental organizations have commenced the practice of soliciting contributions in Bitcoin and various alternative forms of currency. You'll be surprised that some have even started its illicit use, like in some cases of underground online marketplaces that deal with illegal goods.

Cryptocurrencies have gained widespread popularity due to their myriad of advantages when compared to traditional fiat currencies. However, similar to any investment, cryptocurrencies also present certain disadvantages, which we will delve into in subsequent sections.

History of Cryptocurrency

The market was first introduced to the practical applications of cryptocurrencies merely 7 years ago; nevertheless, the technical underpinnings of these digital assets can be traced back to approximately three decades ago, specifically the 1980s.

David Chaum, a renowned cryptographer, is credited with being the pioneer who first conceived the concept of a cryptocurrency. He invented an encrypted computer algorithm that facilitated secure, unalterable exchanges between two parties. Subsequently, he founded one of the earliest enterprises dedicated to manufacturing monetary units using his algorithm, known as the DigiCash. It was the sole corporation with the capability to manufacture the currency, which is regarded as exemplary, distinct from Bitcoin and numerous other cryptocurrencies, wherein anyone with the appropriate computational resources can engage in currency mining.

The corporation announced its filing for bankruptcy during the latter half of the 1990s, subsequent to encountering various legal complications and declining Microsoft's proposition for collaboration. This agreement would have connected DigiCash with each individual Windows operating system installed in households.

Wei Dai, a renowned software engineer from China, authored a seminal research paper on b-money that established the fundamental principles underlying the architecture of contemporary cryptocurrencies. It encompassed details regarding algorithms, the decentralized nature of operations, as well as the anonymity of buyers. The currency failed to materialize.

The adoption of E-gold, a digital currency platform headquartered in the United States, was also not successful during the 1990s. This business was established in the state of Florida. It issued E-gold "tokens" to customers in return for their antique trinkets, jewelry, and coins. These E-gold tokens can be exchanged for US dollars. It enjoyed early success, boasting an excess of 1 million active accounts during the mid-2000s. E-gold allowed for indiscriminate account opening, thereby facilitating the perpetration of fraudulent activities through its platform. The lack of robust security measures resulted in widespread hacking occurrences that ultimately led to the closure of the organization in 2009.

Bitcoin is credited as the progenitor of contemporary cryptocurrencies. The original exposition of this concept was initially attributed to an unidentified figure, the singular or multiple origins of whom remain unverified - Satoshi Nakamoto. Upon the public release of Bitcoin in early 2009, numerous individuals who held a strong interest in the subject commenced the activities of mining, investing, and exchanging this particular form of currency. The inception of the Bitcoin market transpired in February 2010.

In the latter part of 2012, WordPress, a burgeoning hosting and website development platform, established itself as a pioneer among prominent retailers by enabling the acceptance of Bitcoin as a valid form of payment for transactions.

And thus, the subsequent events are widely regarded as pivotal moments that shaped subsequent developments.

Selecting Your Ethereum Wallet

There exists a variety of alternatives available for selection, and one must carefully deliberate upon the characteristics and aesthetics that would most aptly align with their requirements. Experienced traders often assert that there exist wallets that are most suitable for individuals new to trading. If you are dissatisfied with the functionality of your current wallet or if you wish to explore alternative options, you have the option to replace it.

Here are some exemplifications of Ethereum wallets that you can consider:

MetaMask

MetaMask is accessible effortlessly through your browser as an extension due to its web-based nature. It offers convenience for testing purposes due to its ability to establish connections with various test blockchains and Ethereum nodes.

Jaxx

Jaxx is compatible with a wide range of operating systems, including iOS, Android, Linux, Windows, and macOS. This wallet is designed to support multiple currencies and platforms, making it particularly well-suited for individuals who are new to cryptocurrency. It can serve as both a desktop and mobile wallet.

MyEtherWallet (MEW)

MEW is an alternative web-based wallet that can be conveniently accessed through any internet browser. It possesses an array of functionalities that are available for your exploration.

Emerald Wallet

This wallet demonstrates compatibility with both the Ethereum Classic blockchain and various other blockchains. It functions effectively on operating systems such as Windows, Linux, and macOS, owing to its status as an open-source desktop application. One can choose to operate this in its complete mode, or alternatively, one can establish a connection with a publicly accessible remote node. It is accompanied by a complementary tool that facilitates all of its functionalities.

Accessibility

Ethereum grants users the ability to exercise control over their private keys. One private key is equal to one account.

Nevertheless, certain users opt to utilize the services of an external custodian for the management of their private keys. It is crucial to acknowledge that maintaining control entails a significant responsibility. One must acquire the competence to effectively manage and oversee their private keys if one desires to ensure the safeguarding, confidentiality, and integrity of their ethers.

"These suggestions would undoubtedly prove to be beneficial:

Abstain from engaging in experimentation or improvisation when it comes to matters of security. Ensure that you employ dependable strategies.

The utilization of an air-gapped service ensures the attainment of utmost security; nevertheless, it is not obligatory for each individual account.

The higher the significance of your account, the more stringent security measures ought to be implemented.

It is advised not to retain your private key in unencrypted format, particularly in digital form. The majority of contemporary user interfaces incorporate security measures such as encryption to deter unauthorized access and safeguard sensitive data from potential breaches by malicious actors.

Private keys have the capacity to be encrypted, such as through the utilization of a "digital Keystore" file. You will be required to furnish a password in order to gain access to it. For the sake of security, it is crucial to ensure that your password is robust and resistant to unauthorized access. If necessary, you may choose to document it in writing and store it in a secure location that remains exclusively under your control. In order to access it, you will require both your password and Keystore file.

It is strongly advised to refrain from storing any of your passwords in digital files, such as documents, screenshots, photos, or online storage platforms. Use a password manager.

When you are requested to generate a mnemonic word sequence as a means of backing up a key, a redundant physical backup is also retained. It is highly recommended not to postpone that specific task as there is a high likelihood of it slipping from memory. These backups can be utilized to reconstruct your private key in the event of complete loss of data or password misplacement. However, it is important to note that hackers might exploit your private keys as well. Therefore, it is recommended to maintain a physical, written version of your private key or password. Keeping it securely locked away in a drawer or in a place known only to you remains the most advisable course of action.

When conducting the transfer of substantial amounts of ETH, especially to a newly generated address, it is advisable to perform an initial test transaction, such as a transaction of $1, and subsequently await the issuance of a confirmation receipt.

Prior to establishing a new account, it is advised to initially initiate test transactions of nominal value towards the new address. Once you have obtained a confirmation receipt, you may proceed with returning it from the corresponding account. There is a possibility of encountering issues during the creation of a new account, hence it is advisable to conduct a trial transaction. This will additionally serve to verify the effectiveness of the process.

Utilizing a publicly accessible blockchain explorer enables one to ascertain the acceptance status of a transaction. However, this could potentially compromise your privacy as divulging your address to block explorers allows for easy tracking of your movements.

Investing In Stablecoins

On October 31st, 2020, a considerable duration had elapsed since the dissemination of the Bitcoin white paper by Satoshi Nakamoto, marking a significant period of transformative developments. Numerous potential crypto initiatives have emerged from a segment of the world's most brilliant individuals. The market capitalization of cryptocurrency is continuously expanding, and Bitcoin is approaching unprecedented peaks. Moreover, the current surge in advancement and investment has sparked enthusiasm among the very entities that cryptocurrencies aim to revolutionize and replace. Governments and corporations worldwide have initiated experimentation with blockchain technologies, although these initiatives do not possess the same characteristics of privacy, security, transparency, decentralization, and freedom that define cryptocurrencies. National banks are now diligently working towards the development of their own digital currencies, while numerous private enterprises are capitalizing on cryptocurrencies by funding their own initiatives, such as the creation of stable coins that are gradually gaining dominance in the crypto market. Clearly, it is evident that these elements are currently not operating in isolation. Therefore, in this section, I will explore some noteworthy connections between USDC, Stellar, the IMF, and their potential impact on the future of digital currency. While conducting research on stable coin issuance, I fortuitously discovered several conspicuous connections among various private and public entities involved in stable coins and analogous technologies, notably Central Bank digital currencies or CBDCs. Although many of these associations are evident and well-documented, there are some that are a bit more speculative. Before I commence drawing connections, I shall extend a preliminary cautionary hypothesis. Perhaps the enigmatic ultimate phase of supporting stable coins with the US dollar is aimed at undermining alternative forms of public currency. This is due to the fact that individuals have the ability to create a temporary US dollar account quickly by using a mobile cryptocurrency wallet that supports stable coins such as USDT or USDC. Consequently, in the event that a different national currency, such as the Euro, experiences rapid depreciation in comparison to the US dollar, stemming from factors like extensive money supply expansion by the European Central Bank in response to the economic consequences of a global pandemic, individuals residing in the Eurozone possess the ability to safeguard their assets by conveniently acquiring USDT or USDC using their debit or credit cards. Moreover, it should be noted that individuals possess the ability to utilize these stable coins within their domestic borders by means of either a physical cryptocurrency debit card or a mobile crypto payment application featuring a virtual NFC card. In the event that this were to happen on a significant scale, it could have a profoundly detrimental impact on the Euro currency. It appears that this concern holds significant legitimacy among state-run administrations worldwide and has been a source of nocturnal distress for numerous years. This phenomenon is referred to as dollarization, wherein there is a complete or partial substitution of domestic currency with the United States dollar. The concept of dollarization was analyzed in a series of lectures conducted by the International Monetary Fund on October 19th in relation to cross-border payments. The International Monetary Fund, headquartered in Washington DC, endeavors to facilitate the monetary policies of over 190 nations to ensure global economic stability and prosperity. Consequently, they possess a distinct inclination towards engaging in activities involving money-printing devices. The courses offered by the IMF on October 19th were centered around a comprehensive framework for the effective revitalization of currency. Presented are the facts: nations and financial institutions globally are presently acutely aware that their monopoly on currency is being threatened. Curiously, it was not cryptocurrencies that triggered the alarm. It was Facebook's Libra. This is due to the fact that Facebook possesses a vast user base. Approximately half of the overall population is utilizing Facebook or a platform owned by Facebook such as WhatsApp or Instagram. This indicates that Libra has the potential to achieve widespread acceptance in the near future. Governments, to a certain extent, do not perceive cryptocurrencies as a significant threat, which explains why the same cannot be asserted for these digital currencies. While Libra faces limitations within judicial proceedings, the International Monetary

Fund is actively endeavoring to assist governmental bodies worldwide in establishing their own solutions to the predicaments they themselves have brought about. This primarily entails establishing a vast network of interconnected CBDC blockchains. Every Central Bank Digital Currency (CBDC) will be produced and supervised by its respective Central Bank, and each will leverage at least one distributed ledger technology to facilitate the transfer of value between users. Every individual engaging with this global Central Bank Digital Currency (CBDC) entity is expected to possess a distinct digital identity, securely stored on a blockchain, accessible to virtually all governmental and central banking authorities worldwide. The International Monetary Fund requires nations across the globe to commence implementing these measures within the upcoming five-year timeframe. This is the location where things become intriguing. It is apparent that the blockchains serving as the foundation for these CVDCs will possess a combination of private and public attributes. Public blockchains encompass the integration of digital currency blockchains. Danelle Dixon, CEO of Stellar, and Rennie Reinsberg, CEO of Cello, were the two experts selected to participate in one of the workshops organized by the International Monetary Fund (IMF). Given your level of awareness regarding updates on digital currency, it is probable that you were already aware of this information. The manner in which two digital currency projects were handled during a significant event by a global organization, concerned with financial management, may elicit some Fear of Missing Out (FOMO). However, this alone does not definitively indicate that these or any other cryptocurrency endeavors will be chosen to contribute to the development of an admittedly

tragic future. In order to substantiate our argument, additional evidence will be needed. Jerome Powell holds the position of the Chairman of the Federal

Reserve, the prominent institution responsible for implementing vital monetary policies that shape the economic landscape of the United States. In the event that I were to be preoccupied by a singular piece of cryptographic news, it would be the revelation that the Federal Reserve currently possesses no intentions to develop a digital currency for the purpose of a Central Bank. The Federal Reserve has consistently provided this response on every occasion they have been questioned, and it was once again reiterated by Jerome Powell during an IMF session on cross-border payments on October 19, 2020. In the aforementioned seminar, the IMF arbitrator stated that over 80% of global Central Banks possess intentions to develop a Central Bank Digital Currency (CBDC). The US dollar serves as not only the official currency of the largest economy globally, but also as the world's reserve currency. Simply put, the United States dollar also serves as the stable currency of sovereign-issued currencies.

In my perspective, there exist only two rationales for the Federal Reserve to assert that they do not intend to create a central bank digital currency (CBDC). It is conceivable that they are cognizant of the potential disclosure of significant levels of corruption that would inevitably arise from the widespread adoption of CBDCs, or perhaps a variation of a dollar CBDC is already in existence. Although the primary explanation is undeniably plausible, it is impractical for me to provide a demonstrable proof for it. Furthermore, it surpasses the boundaries of this book. What I aim to illustrate nevertheless is that an equivalent to a CBDC already exists, and I believe it to be the USDC. Although Tether may hold the distinction of being the largest stable coin in terms of market capitalization, it is worth noting that USDC is currently experiencing the most rapid growth among stablecoins in the cryptocurrency sphere. This is because of several factors. Primarily, it is important to ascertain whether Circle possesses the requisite amount of US dollars that are readily accessible for the purpose of facilitating the transfer and utilization of USDC. Contrarily, Tether diverges in that it maintains an equivalent measure to the US dollar within its USDT cryptocurrency; however, the backing is not in physical US dollars, but rather in a basket of assets that includes loans extended to affiliated companies. Furthermore, in the year 2019, Circle collaborated with Coinbase, the preeminent cryptocurrency exchange in the United States, and jointly established the Center Consortium, with a primary focus on the advancement and widespread adoption of USDC. Prior to the conclusion of 2019, Circle had divested all its services with the aim of exclusively dedicating efforts towards the development of USDC. This entailed the sale of the Polonex cryptocurrency exchange, which they acquired in 2018, and the divestment of their profitable OTC trading service to Kraken. A publication on the Medium platform written by Circle explores this practice in-depth, concluding with the following remark:

The global surge in stable coins and digital currencies backed by Central Bank reserves, coupled with the emergence of third-generation public blockchains and the accelerated global interest in cryptocurrencies, collectively create a remarkable backdrop for the introduction of our new platform services in 2020. In August 2020, the Center Consortium unveiled USDC 2.0, which enables the transmission of USDC on the Ethereum network without incurring any gas fees. Taking all factors into account, it follows that the payment for that gas is thus made in USDC. USDC 2.0 also introduced a new implementation of on-chain multiple signature contracts, incorporating innovative contract mechanisms. Approximately one month later, the Office of the Comptroller of the Currency (OCC) granted permission to federally chartered banks to offer banking services to stablecoin issuers. Please take note that this declaration represents a significant departure from the stance taken by the OCC in July, wherein government banks were granted approval to administer digital currency assets. Evidently, the US government is seeking to promote the development of stable coins, and I firmly believe this is not because they desire individuals to yield farming in DeFi protocols. I believe this intends to foster competition among stablecoin guarantors in order to determine the most suitable candidate for launching a central bank digital currency (CBDC). Moreover, USDC is undoubtedly regarded as the undisputed dominant leader, at least for the time being. USDC differs significantly from a potential US dollar CBDC; it is issued by a centralized authority, subject to its control, and operates as a digital store of value, whereby each token possesses a distinct identifier and transaction record. Both Coinbase and Circle have also displayed to us professionals their willingness and preparedness to take action. Coinbase has a history of suspending their clients' assets. On their website, it is indicated that they undertake such measures in compliance with legal obligations and also in accordance with less stringent regulations set forth by various US regulatory bodies, such as the Office of Foreign Assets Control. The circle has also implemented a freeze on wallets that previously held USDC, and the new boycotting strategy from Center signifies that USDC adheres to a comparable approach as Coinbase. Such an outcome should not come as a surprise, given that the Center Consortium comprises both Circle and Coinbase. All of these factors indicate to me that USDC has the potential to evolve into the Central Bank Digital Currency (CBDC) of the United States. Currently, the sole matter that remains is determining the blockchain on which it will ultimately reside. Government entities and central banking institutions worldwide have been actively pursuing optimal blockchain solutions for their forthcoming central bank digital currencies (CBDCs). They are contemplating the incorporation of both private and public blockchains, including those specifically designed for digital currency. Prominent entities operating in the private sector, such as Microsoft, Mastercard, JP Morgan, and even PayPal, have expressed their interest and participation in the potential implementation of Central Bank Digital Currency (CBDC). Immediately, it seems highly unlikely that any governmental authority or Central Bank would opt for a digital currency blockchain over a private blockchain provided by one of these well-established entities. However, digital currency blockchains possess a distinct advantage over private blockchains: genuine competition. To ascertain the status of the engine's operations

Unless you come across a select number of superior-grade blockchain presentations developed by a technological behemoth such as Google, your chances of success would be quite limited. Virtually all of their blockchains are proprietary, taking all factors into account. A potential competitor such as Amazon has the ability to replicate the strategy, enhance it to a greater degree, obtain a patent for it, and safeguard it through a stack of confidentiality agreements. On the other hand, it is worth noting that practically every cryptocurrency blockchain is available in open-source format. This suggests that in order to maintain a competitive edge, one must continually advance at a rapid pace. The demand for a blockchain in the cryptocurrency domain that is considerably faster, significantly more decentralized, and notably safer is exceedingly pronounced. Everybody is watching,

including the opposition. Similarly, a significant portion of these individuals who are creating these blockchains fail to take the necessary steps in order to earn money quickly. A multitude of cryptographic engineers are earnestly endeavoring to develop a blockchain system capable of facilitating the future of currency envisioned by Satoshi Nakamoto. Certain individuals, akin to insurance coin developers, devote their efforts to their projects based solely on the principles they personally uphold. It is highly probable that looking after them would pose a challenge. Engineering professionals at renowned organizations such as Google and Facebook are generously remunerated, provided with complimentary meals, afforded comfortable sleeping quarters, offered limited housing options, facilitated with complimentary transportation to and from their workplace, and even granted access to various recreational facilities within the premises. In the meantime, Andre Cronier, who appears to be facing significant setbacks, occupies a modestly air-conditioned workspace in an undisclosed location in South Africa, working diligently to construct DeFi protocols. Why? Given that his motivation primarily stems from interior sources rather than external influences, such as those commonly observed among developers in Silicon Valley. Based on all the aforementioned factors, it is my belief that the United States will opt for a digital currency blockchain platform to develop a blockchain for their Central Bank Digital Currency (CBDC). In any event, which alternative shall we choose? Taking into account every factor, all indicators point to Stellar. Throughout the preceding year, the middle consortium has actively pursued the most optimal blockchain for their USDC stablecoin. In June, they announced their intention to deploy USDC on the Algorand blockchain, followed by the subsequent disclosure in October of plans to integrate USDC with

Stellar and Solana, thereby expanding the number of supported blockchains. In addition, Heavenly was one of the cryptocurrency initiatives discussed during the IMF's latest discourse on cross-border payments. In the course of this conversation, Danelle Dixon, the CEO of Stellar, observed the imperative need for Stellar to align and integrate with the existing financial framework instead of displacing it entirely. Furthermore, Dixon recognized that USDC serves as the crucial catalyst for facilitating the adoption of Central Bank Digital Currencies (CBDCs). Such astute recognition is particularly noteworthy, given the recent collaboration between Stellar and the esteemed consortium. Furthermore, the presence of another encounter involving Stellar and the Federal Reserve has led me to ascertain that there is a considerable amount of undisclosed activity occurring backstage.

In the month of March 2019, Jed McCaleb, co-founder of Stellar, delivered a discourse to Michael Warner, a senior analyst at the Federal Reserve.

The Bank of San Francisco entered into a shared phase. They were in close proximity to each other. This dialogue essentially consolidates all the aforementioned points in this section, specifically emphasizing the necessity for the Federal Reserve to engage a private enterprise in the development of the blockchain infrastructure that will support their Central Bank Digital Currency (CBDC). Moreover, it highlights Stellar's desire to collaborate with the Federal Reserve in order to provide said blockchain. The experts thoroughly examined the precise elements of competition that I previously mentioned in the preceding section. Indicating that it will essentially culminate in an unceasing confrontation among blockchains vying for supremacy in the realm of central bank digital currencies. Michael Warner just indicated comprehension. Additionally, it noteworthy to mention that at a certain point during the conversation, Michael Warner directs his attention towards Jed and inquires about his perspective on the methodology behind developing a Central Bank Digital Currency (CBDC) on the Stellar blockchain platform. Heavenly has caught the attention of the Federal Reserve. That much is self-evident. In my opinion, it is highly likely that the United States' Central Bank Digital Currency (CBDC) will be established using USDC as its foundation and built upon a potentially proprietary and selectively-permissioned blockchain platform developed by Stellar. Taking all factors into consideration, it can be concluded that the USDC has not yet been launched on the Stellar platform.

Acknowledging that this approach effectively convinces states and central banks that their collaborative technology is sufficiently robust for domestic and international use, my previous hypothesis may indeed come to fruition. Before bringing this case to a close, there is one remaining aspect that must be addressed, and that pertains to the anticipated timeline for the implementation of a Central Bank Digital Currency (CBDC) in the United States. An additional hypothesis warranting caution pertains to the United States' lack of enthusiasm towards the adoption of Central Bank Digital Currency (CBDC), which can be attributed to the following rationale. Several less affluent countries are currently deploying their own central bank digital currencies as a means of safeguarding their economies from the dominance of the US dollar. Chinese authorities have recently expressed that the implementation of the Digital One currency serves as a safeguard against the prevalence of dollarization. This suggests that, with regards to virtually all nations apart from the United States, central bank digital currencies (CBDCs) are not viewed as an ultimate goal, but rather as an unavoidable compromise. Furthermore, this outcome provides protection against the process of dollarization. The Central Bank Digital Currency (CBDC) holds significant potential as a strategic tool for the United States. Depending on the strategic implementation, it has the potential to trigger widespread dollarization that many countries are striving to safeguard themselves against. Why not initiate the creation now as various nations are still in the process of assembling? Considering the United States' evident pursuit of an economic rivalry with various nations, the development of a Central Bank Digital Currency (CBDC) could be likened to a strategic weapon akin to the nuclear bomb during the resulting global conflict. Taking everything into consideration, it can be noted that US dollar stable coins such as USDT and USDC are progressing steadily, primarily driven not by individuals seeking hedge positions while trading cryptocurrencies or aiming to profit from highly lucrative DeFi returns. They are increasingly being employed for the purpose of transferring surplus across international borders, particularly in the East Asian region, with a particular focus on China. According to Chain Analysis, stable coins are only surpassed by Bitcoin as the cryptocurrency utilized for cross-border transactions. This holds true for every continent. The value of the cryptocurrency in terms of the US dollar is

Annually, an astronomical amount of goods is transported across international boundaries, reaching into the billions. A significant departure from the approximate figure of 200 trillion units of currency that routinely traverse international boundaries through officially issued means. Regrettably, the report by Chain Analysis fails to address the potential transformation of stable coins into the preferred cryptocurrency method for cross-border payments. If by any chance they are, their utilization may indeed begin to rival fiat payments in the coming years. In the eventuality of such a circumstance, it would lead to the implementation of dollarization. In my opinion, that is an innovative and groundbreaking strategy. "Governments and central banks worldwide are exercising patience in developing their

CBDCs, with a few exceptions. This cautious approach is likely driven by the perception that the US government and the Federal Reserve have also been slow to progress in this area. In the interim, the United States is not inconspicuously facilitating favorable conditions for privately owned companies within its jurisdiction to expand and dominate other currencies by utilizing US dollar stable coins. The adoption of stable coins denominated in US dollars is consistently increasing, while concurrently witnessing advancements in their efficacy and the underlying blockchain technology they rely on. Why should there be a rush, given that government authorities currently maintain oversight and possess a certain degree of control over the entities responsible for issuing these stablecoins? There is a potential scenario where stable coins denominated in US dollars may undermine existing public monetary standards. In such a case, the immediate necessity for a central bank digital currency (CBDC) tied to the US dollar might not be as critical. Alternatively, other nations may eventually establish their own CBDCs. The US government could simply choose to either acquire duplicates or provide assurance for USDC and its underlying blockchain as their official Central Bank Digital Currency (CBDC). Once the day arrives when the US government selects the stablecoin sponsor and blockchain for their central bank digital currency (CBDC), it is highly probable that they will possess a significant efficiency advantage over other CBDCs, thereby establishing a substantial lead in this area. We express our profound appreciation for the tremendous encouragement and collaboration provided by the unrestricted economy competition. Therefore, this would establish the computerized US dollar as the preferred currency worldwide, thereby resulting in the adoption of dollarization. The majority of what I alluded to in this section is based on conjecture. However, it is my belief that several aspects are undoubtedly evident. Countries across the globe are endeavoring to introduce their own sophisticated digital currencies through their respective Central Banks. They are actively seeking stablecoin supporters to aid them in nurturing the technology, as well as seeking partnerships with established companies and public blockchains to bolster the development of the envisioned global interoperable blockchain network. In my professional opinion, it is highly likely that the United States will select the Center Consortium stablecoin innovation and Stellar's blockchain innovation as the foundation for their Central Bank Digital Currency (CBDC). There is substantial evidence of interconnectivity among these disparate assemblies, however, this does not imply that the present leaders can alter their course in the future. This aspect has the potential to undergo alteration upon your perusal of this literary work. However, it seems that the United States is not experiencing a significant increase in the usage of their Central Bank Digital Currency (CBDC). I believe this is the case due to the dollarization they wish to attain.

Delineating this phenomenon, one can observe the nascent emergence of stable coins linked to the US dollar. Experts from the United States have identified the optimal environment for competitors in stable coin guarantor and blockchain organizations to contend for supremacy. This would effectively ensure the continued expansion of US dollar stable coins, while various governmental bodies strive to launch their respective Central Bank Digital Currencies (CBDCs). In due course, when the time arrives, the United States will possess the most advanced CBDC technology within close reach. When can we expect the arrival of the Central Bank Digital Currency? Based on the indication provided by the IMF gauge, a reasonable timeframe of 5 to 10 years can be considered, and it is expected that the United States will be among the last countries to adopt this measure.

Systems For Identity And Reputation

The initial decentralized digital currency, known as Namecoin, sought to leverage a blockchain structure similar to Bitcoin in order to establish a system for name registration. This innovative platform allows users to register their names within a publicly accessible database alongside additional information. The primary utilized scenario pertains to a DNS system, which facilitates the translation of domain names such as "bitcoin.org" (or, in the context of Namecoin, "bitcoin.bit") into corresponding IP addresses. Additional applications encompass email authentication as well as potentially more sophisticated reputation systems. Presented herewith is the fundamental agreement to facilitate an Ethereum-based name registration system similar to Namecoin.

if !contract.storage[tx.data[0]]:

The contract storage at the index "tx.data[0]" is set to be equal to "tx.data[1]".

The contract is exceedingly straightforward, consisting solely of a database residing within the Ethereum network. This database can only be augmented but cannot be altered or removed. Any individual has the ability to enroll a name of significance, which subsequently becomes permanently affixed in the registration. A name registration agreement of higher sophistication will also encompass a 'function clause' that permits other contracts to make inquiries, along with a mechanism for the 'owner' (i.e. the registrant) to... The initial registrar responsible for modifying the data or transferring ownership of a name. One could also incorporate reputation and web-of-trust functionality as an additional feature.

File Storage with a Decentralized Approach

In recent years, several online file storage startups, notably Dropbox, have emerged with the aim of enabling users to upload a backup of their hard drive and entrust the service with storing the backup for a recurring monthly fee, thereby granting users access to it. Nonetheless, presently the market for file storage exhibits occasional inefficiency; a preliminary examination of various existing solutions reveals that, particularly within the "uncanny valley" range of 20-200 GB where neither complimentary quotas nor enterprise-level discounts come into play, the monthly prices for mainstream file storage costs are such that you end up paying more than the cost of an entire hard drive in a single month. Ethereum contracts have the potential to facilitate the creation of a decentralized file storage ecosystem, wherein individual users have the opportunity to generate modest financial gains by leasing their personal hard drives. Furthermore, the surplus of unused storage capacity can be leveraged to effectively reduce the expenses associated with file storage.

The fundamental component of such a device would be what we have referred to as the "contract for decentralized Dropbox." This contract operates in the following manner. Initially, the desired data is partitioned into segments, with encryption measures applied to each segment to ensure confidentiality. Additionally, a Merkle tree is constructed using these encrypted segments. One then establishes a contractual agreement whereby, after every N blocks, the contract selects a random index in the Merkle tree (utilizing the previous block hash, accessible from the contract code, as a source of randomness). X eth is then allocated to the initial entity to provide a transaction accompanied by a simplified payment verification-like proof of ownership of the block at that specific index in the tree. When a user desires to retrieve their file again, they can utilize a micro-payment channel protocol (for example, One could utilize a rate of 1 Szabo per 32 kilobytes to successfully retrieve the file. The most cost-effective approach is for the payer to refrain from publishing the transaction until its conclusion, opting instead to replace the transaction with a slightly more financially advantageous one featuring the same nonce after every 32 kilobytes.

An important aspect of the protocol lies in the fact that, despite the need to trust numerous random nodes to not forget the file, one can greatly mitigate this risk by dividing the file into multiple fragments using secret sharing techniques. By monitoring the contracts, one can ensure that each fragment remains securely held by at least one node. If a contract continues to disburse funds, it serves as a cryptographic evidence that there exists an entity that is actively retaining the file.

Decentralized Autonomous Organizations (DAOs)

The overarching concept of a "decentralized organization" pertains to a virtual entity characterized by a specific group of members or shareholders who, potentially with a majority of 67%, possess the authority to allocate the entity's resources and amend its governing principles. The organization would ascertain the appropriate allocation of its funds through collective decision-making by its members. Possible mechanisms for distributing a DAO's funds encompass a spectrum of options, spanning from rewards and remuneration to more intricate systems like the utilization of an internal currency to incentivize contributions. This essentially emulates the legal entanglements typically observed in a conventional company or nonprofit, solely relying on cryptographic blockchain technology for enforcement. Thus far, a significant portion of the discourse surrounding Decentralized Autonomous Organizations (DAOs) has centered around the concept of a "capitalist" model referred to as a "Decentralized Autonomous Corporation" (DAC), wherein shareholders receive dividends and tradable shares. An alternative approach, possibly characterized as a "decentralized autonomous community," would ensure that all members have an equal say in decision-making and require a consensus of 67% of existing members to approve the addition or removal of a member. The stipulation that an individual can possess only one membership would subsequently necessitate collective enforcement by the group.

A general framework for the implementation of a Design Optimization (DO) can be delineated as follows. The most basic design involves a fragment of code that is capable of adapting itself, adjusting its characteristics when a consensus is reached among at least two-thirds of the members regarding a modification. Despite the inherent immutability of code, it is possible to circumvent this limitation and establish de facto mutability by segregating portions of the code into distinct contracts, with the address of these contracts stored in modifiable storage for invocation purposes. "In a basic instantiation of such a decentralized autonomous organization (DAO) contract, three transaction types would exist, distinguished by the data provided within the transaction:

To formally submit a proposal, with index i, for the alteration of the address located at storage index K to the designated value, V.

• In order to record a vote in support of proposal i

• To conclude the proposal and proceed to the next stage, a sufficient number of votes must be garnered.

The contract would subsequently include provisions pertaining to each of these matters. It is intended to keep a comprehensive log of all modifications made to storage that remain accessible, alongside a roster showcasing the individuals who cast their votes in favor of these modifications. Additionally, it would include a comprehensive roster of all members. When any storage change gets to two thirds of members voting for it, a finalizing transaction could execute the change. A more advanced framework would also possess inherent voting capabilities for functions such as conducting transactions, adding and removing members, and may even support the concept of Liquid Democracy-style vote delegation. Individuals have the ability to designate another individual to vote on their behalf, and this act of designation carries over to subsequent designations. For example, if individual A designates individual B, and B then designates individual C, it is C who ultimately determines the voting choice of A. This design would facilitate the organic growth of the DO as a decentralized community, enabling individuals to eventually delegate the responsibility of vetting members to specialists. However, unlike in the current system, specialists can easily enter and exit the community as individual members change their alignments.

A feasible option is the implementation of a decentralized corporate structure, wherein each account holds the potential to possess zero or more shares, and a minimum of two-thirds of these shares is necessary to reach a consensus when making decisions. A comprehensive framework would encompass asset management capabilities, the capacity to initiate a purchase or sale of shares, and the capability to accept offers (preferably with an inherent order-matching mechanism embedded within the contract). Delegation would similarly be structured in a manner resembling Liquid Democracy, thereby extending the application of the concept of a "board of directors".

In the forthcoming era, there is a likelihood of deploying more sophisticated mechanisms to govern organizations; it is at this juncture that it becomes viable to designate a decentralized organization (DO) as a decentralized autonomous organization (DAO). The distinction between a DO and a DAO can be somewhat ambiguous, but it typically hinges on whether the governance is primarily conducted through a political-like procedure or an automated process. A useful measure to assess this differentiation is the criterion of "no common language": can the organization continue to operate effectively even if its members do not share a common language?" A traditional shareholder-oriented corporation would undoubtedly be unsuccessful, whereas a system like the Bitcoin protocol would be considerably more inclined to achieve success. Robin Hanson's futarchy, a mechanism for organizational governance through prediction markets, serves as an excellent representation of what a genuinely "autonomous" governance system could resemble. Please be mindful that it is not advisable to automatically assume that all DAOs are inherently superior to all DOs. Automation is merely a paradigm that is expected to yield substantial advantages in specific contexts, while its practicality may vary in other scenarios. Additionally, it is highly likely that there will also be numerous semi-DAOs in existence.

Further Applications

1. Savings wallets. Let's consider the scenario in which Alice desires to ensure the security of her funds, yet she harbors concerns about potential loss or unauthorized access to her private key. She incorporates the element of ether into a contractual agreement with Bob, who represents a banking institution, in the following manner:

Alice has the exclusive authority to withdraw a maximum of 1% of the funds per day.

• While Bob has the capacity to withdraw no more than 1% of the funds per day, Alice possesses the authority to execute a transaction using her key that effectively disables this capability.

• Alice and Bob have the collective ability to withdraw any amount.

Typically, a daily interest rate of 1% suffices for Alice. In the event that Alice requires a larger withdrawal, she may seek assistance from Bob. In the event that Alice's key is compromised, she seeks assistance from Bob to transfer the funds to a new contract. In the event that she misplaces her key, Bob will ultimately retrieve the funds. In the event that Bob proves to be malevolent, she has the option to disable his capability to make withdrawals.

2. Crop insurance. One could readily engage in a financial derivatives contract by substituting a data feed pertaining to

weather conditions instead of relying on any price index. Should an Iowa farmer choose to acquire a derivative that offers inverse payout dependent on precipitation levels in Iowa, the farmer will receive automatic monetary compensation in the event of a drought. Conversely, if there is a sufficient amount of rain, the farmer will find contentment as their crops thrive.

3. A decentralized data feed. In the realm of financial contracts for difference, it may indeed be plausible to achieve data feed decentralization via a protocol known as "SchellingCoin". The operational concept of SchellingCoin can be summarized as follows: Multiple parties contribute the assigned value of a specific data point into the designated system. The price of ETH/USD is determined, the values are arranged, and individuals falling within the 25th and 75th percentiles will receive one token as a form of reward. All individuals possess the motivation to present the response that aligns with the

consensus, and the sole esteemed consensus that a significant portion of participants can feasibly converge upon is the evident default: the veracity. This establishes a decentralized protocol that has the potential to offer an array of values, such as the exchange rate between ETH and USD, the temperature in Berlin, or even the outcome of a specific complex calculation.

4. Smart multi-signature escrow. Bitcoin facilitates the use of multi-signature transaction contracts whereby, for instance, three out of a total of five keys are required to authorize the expenditure of the funds. Ethereum provides enhanced levels of granularity, exemplified by the ability for four out of five individuals to expend their entire holdings, three out of five individuals to spend up to 10% per day, and two out of five individuals to spend up to 0.5% per day. Furthermore, Ethereum multi-signature functionality operates asynchronously, allowing two parties to record their signatures on the

blockchain at separate instances. The transaction will be automatically executed upon receiving the final signature.

5. Cloud computing. The EVM technology can additionally be employed to establish a verifiable computing environment, enabling users to solicit the execution of computations from others and, if desired, demand evidence of the accurate completion of these computations at specific randomly chosen milestones. This facilitates the emergence of a cloud computing marketplace wherein any user can engage using their desktop, laptop, or dedicated server, and verification mechanisms, accompanied by security deposits, can be employed to guarantee the system's reliability. nodes cannot profitably cheat). Whilst this particular system may not be appropriate for all tasks, those which necessitate extensive inter-process communication, as an illustration, are not easily executable on a substantial cluster of nodes. However,

certain tasks can be parallelized with greater ease. Projects such as SETI@home, Folding@home, and genetic algorithms can be readily implemented on such a platform.

6. Peer-to-peer gambling. Various peer-to-peer gambling protocols, such as the Cybedice protocol developed by Frank Stajano and Richard Clayton, have the potential to be integrated into the Ethereum blockchain. The most rudimentary gambling protocol can be described as a mere contract for difference utilizing the next block hash. From this basic foundation, more sophisticated protocols can be constructed, thereby enabling the development of gambling services characterized by negligible fees and absolute immunity to fraudulent activities.

7. Prediction markets. Prediction markets, given the presence of an oracle or SchellingCoin, are also relatively straightforward to integrate, and their combination with SchellingCoin has the

potential to emerge as the initial prominent implementation of futarchy as a governance protocol for decentralized organizations.

8. In the context of blockchain-based decentralized marketplaces, leveraging the identity and reputation system as a foundational element.

Using Macd Indicators

With a touch of creativity, it is arguable that the MACD indicator resembles the undulating motion of a roller coaster, would you not agree? Robust fluctuations in the market can indeed evoke such sensations! The striking volatility witnessed in cryptocurrency markets can be exceedingly pronounced.

In this segment, we will provide a succinct overview of the Moving Average Convergence Divergence (MACD) indicator. A reliable indicator that offers valuable insights into price fluctuations. We will elucidate the role of hints in facilitating prudent decision-making.

If you are without one, we advise perusing our earlier publications, such as our articles on Portfolio Management, RSI Indicators, Moving Averages, and Bollinger Bands.

What is MACD?

First and foremost, could you kindly provide the definition of MACD?

The acronym MACD denotes the moving average convergence and divergence indicator. In the event that you have perused our article pertaining to Moving Average, you may find these terms to be acquainted.

Henceforth, we shall consider Moving Average Convergence and Divergence in the abbreviated form of MACD. The goal of this segment is to provide an explanation of the MACD in order to facilitate its comprehension and application.

MACD definition

A formal way to say the same thing is: "The Moving Average Convergence and Divergence (MACD) indicator is employed to signify the correlation between velocity and the two moving averages of a given trend." A momentum indicator is intended to provide a comprehensive understanding of the extent to which the market has engaged in buying or selling activities. Convergence and divergence pertain to the visual differentiation between the price and the signal, specifically the moving average of the signal in this particular context. In summary, it denotes the Moving Average Convergence Divergence (MACD) indicator. Remain with us, as this comprehensive guide elucidates the intricacies of the MACD indicator.

How is MACD calculated?

How to calculate MACD? While it is improbable that there will be a necessity for altering the parameters of this indicator or performing MACD computations, it is still advantageous to acquire knowledge of its mathematical principles.

The MACD is calculated by deducting the 26-period Exponential Moving Average (EMA) from the 12-term EMA.

MACD formula

The formula for calculating the Moving Average Convergence Divergence (MACD) is obtained by subtracting the 26-term Exponential Moving Average (EMA) from the 12-term EMA.

Period means candle. When analyzing the daily chart, a single candle within it symbolizes a trade that spans over a period of 24 hours. In this instance, a duration of 12 periods corresponds to a span of 12 days.

How to read MACD?

Now shifting our focus to the primary aspect, let us delve into the intricacies of interpreting the MACD chart.

There is no necessity to modify any configurations; hence, adhering to the fundamental settings would prove most suitable for day trading, long-term investing, or any other engagement with this market that relies on MACD charts.

Once we have activated it within the Good Crypto application, let us deactivate the "roller coaster" indicator.

Please launch the Good Crypto application. Please proceed to the designated trade zone. Upon arrival, proceed to tap the "fx" button in order to gain access to an extensive array of indicators.

We currently possess a balance sheet that includes a daily chart depicting the BTC / USDT rate, along with the MACD indicator.

Please engage in a double-tap action within the gesture field to maximize it to the dimensions of the entire screen. Presently, we are able to observe both the moving averages as well as the histograms. The line in the shade of blue depicts the representation of the 12-month moving average, while the line in the shade of red symbolizes the 26-month moving average.

We have provided elucidation regarding the moving average computation earlier; however, could you please clarify the concept of histogram? The histogram demonstrates the disparity or gap between the two moving averages. The histogram depicts the magnitude of difference between the two moving averages. The histogram reveals the extent of separation between the two moving averages.

MACD Crypto functions

The MACD indicator employs the criteria of a 12 and 26 period moving average. These parameters remain unchanged and it is advisable to maintain them in their current state. Please be advised that signals tend to function more effectively when they are perceived by the majority of individuals. Therefore, it would be prudent to consistently maintain the bitcoin MACD crypto configurations at 12 for the shorter-term moving average and 26 for the longer-term moving average.

This implies that any MACD indicator viewed will be identical. Binary MACD exhibits resemblances to Cracken MACD, while Ethereum MACD demonstrates similarities to Amazon Stock MACD, and so forth.

How to use MACD?

Having a comprehensive comprehension of the MACD indicator is crucial in order to effectively observe the signal and engage in trading activities.

Upon analysis of the moving average, it becomes readily apparent that a crossover has occurred. These factors will serve as essential elements in the application of the MACD indicator.

In conducting MACD technical analysis, one can easily determine the occurrence of selling and buying signals by observing the crossover dynamics.

When the blue line dips beneath the red line, it indicates a signal to purchase. When the ascending movement of the red line crosses above the blue line, it triggers a sell indication.

It serves as a significant determinant of the association and divergence observed between MACD and the price of the asset.

Bitcoin (BTC) and Ethereum (ETH) MACD Strategies for Cryptocurrency Trading

Numerous seasoned technical analysts have encountered or utilized MACD trading on at least one occasion. This indicator has consistently demonstrated its credibility and utility, proving its efficacy on numerous occasions.

Similar to any strategy, the incorporation of appropriate portfolio management and accountability is imperative for the MACD strategy. Nonetheless, no single strategy can be deemed infallible at all times.

The MACD histogram and the intersection points.

What precisely constitutes a MACD histogram? As illustrated previously, the histogram represents the disparity between the two moving averages. Allow me to elucidate the method of deciphering the MACD histogram.

The crossover observed in moving averages is also reflected in the MACD histogram crossover. Utilizing the MACD histogram strategy, incorporating the MACD indicator, proves to be a fundamental yet remarkably efficient approach for discerning opportune moments to execute selling or buying actions. It implies that the trading strategy for the MACD histogram relies on the same crossover pattern indicated by the moving averages.

Executing trades based on the MACD histogram presents a relatively manageable endeavor. Please examine the existing chart and locate the point at which the lines intersect.

Upon the intersection of moving averages, the histogram shall also align accordingly. Denote a modification in the rate at which crossovers occur. Afterwards, we shall examine the price chart and the corresponding indicators to cultivate a comprehensive understanding.

The vertical lines illustrate the precise moment at which the MACD crossing occurred. The initial three crosses can be delineated in the subsequent manner: initially bearish, then profoundly abrupt, and ultimately bearish once more. The most pronounced bearish price movement is evident in the fourth indicator and the final crossover depicted on the daily chart of BTC/USD. From the instant of traversing to the width of the vessel, there was an approximate decrease of 50%.

Crossover constitutes a significant juncture wherein buyers or sellers alter their respective market positions. Similar to a pendulum, velocity oscillates between variations of speed, either rapid or sluggish.

If you recall our previous RSI article, you will observe a discernible contrast between the MACD histograms depicted in the aforementioned example.

MACD Divergence

The Moving Average Convergence Divergence (MACD) suggests instances of both convergence and divergence.

As a point of emphasis, it is important to note that convergence and divergence refer to visual distinctions observed between the price and the indicator, specifically when considering the dynamic average of the indicator in this particular instance.

Depending on the nature of the divergence exhibited by the MACD, we may observe either a bearish MACD divergence or a blush MACD divergence.

Additionally, there is the possibility of a bearish convergence and bearish divergence.

What are the key considerations in formulating a MACD divergence trading strategy? To comprehend this, it is imperative to gain insight into the manner in which the occurrence of bearish divergence or bullish divergence in MACD transitions to MACD.

Consider it from this perspective; the momentum indicator serves as a gauge of the strength behind price fluctuations. The velocity of the price signifies that it is being propelled in a particular direction with considerable magnitude. The velocity will transition from bullish to bearish, or vice versa, at a specific juncture.

The historical background of these movements is provided by the MACD indicator. Each instance of high velocity, whether it be negative or positive, serves as the outermost point of the signal. The magnitudes of acceleration and deceleration surpass or fall beneath the indicated level. These upper and lower elements denote the level of velocity intensity.

As an illustration, when a sequence of peaks exhibits a downward pattern, the velocity diminishes. Conversely, when a sequence of valleys demonstrates an upward trend, the velocity intensifies.

What is the current trading value of MACD? This entails the analysis of the trend's trajectory and strength while juxtaposing it with the price movement, observing for any signs of divergence or convergence.

Moreover, the MACD Divergence Indicator is employed to juxtapose the velocity aforementioned with the fluctuations in market prices.

In this instance of BTC / USDT, there is no favorable divergence observed in the MACD indicator, as it is declining while the price is ascending. Considering the presence of LL-HL for price and LL-LL for oscillator signals suggesting a buying opportunity, the situation could potentially be interpreted as exhibiting positive divergence. However, it is observed on this chart that the magnitude of power at the upper end is larger in comparison to the lower ends. In light of the aforementioned example, it demonstrates a higher tendency attributed to this factor. Typically, it establishes a pathway for the fusion of signals.

The distinction arises when there is a fluctuation in price, whether upwards or downwards, while the corresponding indicator concurrently exhibits a decline. Convergence takes place when the price exhibits a downward movement while the indicator demonstrates an upward or downward movement.

In this particular instance of the MATIC/USD trading pair, a bearish signal can be observed as there is a notable discrepancy between the elevated price and the relatively diminished reading on the MACD indicator. The departure from the norm ceased, and the price experienced an ascent from $1.6 to $1.3.

The final example illustrates a potential situation that may arise. A discerning trader will observe that a divergence arises when the price exhibits an upward trajectory while the MACD exhibits a downward trajectory. Hence, should the trader adhere to chart analysis and indicators, the trader gains knowledge that a desirable scenario entails the MACD exhibiting an upward trend, signifying the market's sustained strength and continuous trajectory. An observation of a downturn in the MACD would signify a state of vulnerability and the potential for a shift towards purchasing.

Note:

HH = higher.

HL is approximately or roughly equivalent to

LH in this context refers to low altitude.

LL = less

MACD vs. RSI Trading Strategy

The trading strategies involving MACD and RSI, which rely on the concepts of Divergence and Convergence, exhibit notable similarities. As you might have observed, both indicators display identical velocity. As a result of this, it is frequently viable to employ the identical uncomplicated MACD trading strategy for other indicators such as RSI.

The optimal approach for day trading using MACD is to initiate trades following the occurrence of highly probable crossovers. When conducting a comparative analysis between RSI and MACD, it becomes evident that MACD possesses the inherent advantage of accurately detecting these crossovers, thereby facilitating a clear visualization of the reversal in momentum.

MACD vs. Stochastic Trading Strategy

Despite the tendency for many individuals to perceive them as synonymous, the MACD and Stochastic indicators exhibit discernible dissimilarities. The stock indicator derives its value from the rate of change in price. The moving average can be expressed as the arithmetic mean of all preceding price values. The stochastic indicator operates as a momentum indicator and, therefore, does not possess the capability to accurately discern the prevailing trend.

Similar to the RSI indicator, the MACD does not provide an accurate trading setup, such as Bollinger Bands or Moving Average, as it is an indicator that is represented within its own framework. Therefore, these candles/price movements are not promptly suspended.

Moreover, apart from this drawback, the MACD indicator possesses significant efficacy and commands considerable reverence among traders. The act of keeping the price chart separate ensures its clarity while continuing to offer valuable insights into market momentum.

Prior to initiating the trade, it is advisable to access the MACD indicator and carefully examine the information that can be gleaned from it. By adhering to this guide, you will be able to interpret any significant signals with clarity.

Engage in cryptocurrency trading using the Moving Average Convergence Divergence (MACD) indicator

Good Crypto is a mobile cryptographic trading terminal that offers traders with top-notch cryptographic trading tools available in the market. By consolidating all of your exchange accounts into a single platform, it enables you to engage in trading activities on the go, while also providing access to a wide range of cryptocurrency markets.

All commercial exchanges and transactions are consolidated within a streamlined portfolio. Progress is monitored chronologically, and the information is accurately presented. In the application, users have the opportunity to explore over 20,000 markets across a span of 30 exchanges. Categorizing these markets based on their performance will enable you to identify the most promising cryptocurrencies and tokens and engage in trading within their respective markets.

Enabling price alerts enables you to receive them in real-time when they are available. Good Crypto additionally furnishes users with fresh notifications, encompassing novel exchange listings, daily market analyses, and notable fluctuations in prices.

When engaging in trading activities, you have the option to extend beyond the conventional formats of exchange orders. The application's design enables the creation of an infinite number of orders without causing any freezing of your account balance. Upon the completion of an order, it is possible to integrate a Stop Loss Order and a Tech Profit Order. Additionally, a trailing stop order has the potential to yield substantial gains by diligently tracking the prevailing trend to its maximum extent.

The Blockchain

The ingenuity of the entire concept lies in its operational mechanics. Cryptography employs sophisticated mathematical algorithms to generate distinct combinations of characters that cannot be fabricated with the intention of appearing genuine. The string of characters is composed of two distinct elements. The initial component pertains exclusively to the specific currency denomination. Consider, if you will, the dollar bill nestled within your pocket. Upon careful examination, a discernible serial number can be observed to be printed on it. The numerical value is distinct, and without painstakingly replicating both the design and printing methods employed on the currency, the usability of the serial number is severely limited. However, it is widely acknowledged that in contemporary times, notes can be easily reproduced. In contrast to Bitcoin, for instance, one can observe the presence of a verified ownership through the serial number of the coin.

Upon the establishment of an account (accessible to all, referred to as a wallet), sole proprietorship is granted to the account holder for the purpose of initiating outgoing fund transfers. Individuals have the ability to deposit funds into this account, yet solely the account owner holds authority to withdraw funds from it. Once the funds are deposited into the wallet, the serial number of the coin undergoes a complete transformation. Therefore, should Mr. A transfer a coin to Ms. B, the complete alphanumeric serial number associated with the coin will then undergo modification to indicate the change in ownership.

We shall examine the intricate explanations and pertinent locations within the corresponding section of the book at a subsequent time. At present, it suffices to be aware that the full number comprises two distinct components. The first one denotes the account number of the owner, while the second one refers to the string that serves as the identification for the specific coin. When the coin is possessed by Mr. A, it assumes the attributes associated with both the coin and Mr. A's account. When he transfers possession of that coin to Ms. B, the coin undergoes a complete transformation—disassociating itself from his account information and assuming the identity associated with her account.

Technology

The system's advantageous feature lies in the fact that the account now possesses exclusive ownership of funds that are impervious to theft. Unlike cash, which does not provide a means to establish ownership in the event of theft, there exists no definitive method to ascertain that the stolen cash belongs to the victim of the robbery. Within the realm of cryptocurrencies, effectuating such a transfer of ownership is deemed virtually unattainable, unless the apparatus that hosted the account itself were to be compromised.

If one comprehends the aforementioned concept, the subsequent query that would naturally arise is, "By what means does the coin alter its string, and who assumes the responsibility of monitoring such changes?"

Once more, that is the brilliance of the system. Allow me to address the latter aspect of that inquiry initially. The entire system's infrastructure is established upon a technology known as the blockchain. The blockchain is a network composed of all the users within the system who are interconnected through a peer-to-peer architecture. Do you recall the music-sharing platform Napster that emerged roughly two decades ago? It functioned as a decentralized networking system and offered a means to distribute musical files. It garnered immense popularity, attracting a diverse range of individuals who converged to exchange an extensive array of musical content and preferences.

The procedure involved placing the desired content into a designated folder on your computer and subsequently initiating the download of the Napster peer-to-peer software. The software would subsequently connect to an online platform and integrate with a network where all other participants were connected. And everyone kept track of what was in everyone else's folder. Therefore, should you desire to acquire the song "Fly me to the Moon" performed by Frank Sinatra, employing a search function would enable you to access a comprehensive inventory of all the computers within the peer-to-peer network housing said file. You were simply required to select the desired source for the download, and upon clicking on it, an immediate connection between your computer and the designated device would be established, facilitating the transfer of files to your system.

Within the context of that overarching conceptual framework, the blockchain consists of individual account holders who maintain active instances of their Bitcoin client on their personal computers. When they become part of the network, the program will establish connections with a predetermined set of nodes (which can be conceptualized as peers). They are not required to establish connections with all of the current nodes. Instead, they only need to connect with a limited number of nodes, which are randomly selected based on the wallet you possess and the settings you have selected. The purpose of this connection to the other nodes is to retrieve all the data residing on the other node and establish a continuous communication channel with it, actively monitoring for any updates.

Simultaneously, there exist additional nodes that shall establish connections with you and derive benefit from the information you possess regarding the client. Their intent is not primarily focused on ascertaining the specific amount of BTC present on your computer, but rather on determining whether you possess the most up-to-date collection of information. In the event that you possess more recent information than what they possess, they will proceed to replicate this information while simultaneously verifying the acquisition of supporting information from an alternative source.

This entire process occurs at a rapid pace, with each new transaction being meticulously documented and subsequently distributed to all the various nodes across the globe. In due course, the entirety of information pertaining to any given transaction becomes accessible across all nodes.

By utilizing diverse algorithms, it becomes feasible to track the trajectory of a coin. You will remain informed regarding the time of transfer, the duration of storage, and the activation status of the account responsible for housing it. However, what you shall remain unaware of is the true identity of the individual in possession of the coin. Nonetheless, you will be privy to all other information. There is a significant amount of transparency in the system and a significant amount of security.

At present, the sheer abundance of nodes in existence renders it exceedingly arduous to engage in counterfeiting or fabricating inaccurate records within the system.

Dangers inherent in the implementation of the Blockchain technology

There exist substantial hazards associated with the blockchain technology, whether it be the original version devised for BTC or any subsequent iterations that emanate from it. Throughout the duration of BTC's existence, it has been pronounced comatose or deceased on over one hundred and fifty occasions. However, throughout each instance, Bitcoin has consistently demonstrated resilience and rejuvenation. Out of the total occurrences nearing one hundred and fifty (to be precise, there have been more, but I have chosen to omit certain cases which I perceive as lacking validity for inclusion in this publication), a subset of these instances has arisen due to attempted theft, hacking, governmental interference, and related factors. However, the coin's popularity has consistently rebounded on each occasion.

Why? Due to the fact that the fundamental group sustaining the market, including not only those who stand to benefit from its presence, but also the unwavering participants who depend on it and assert that fiat currencies are approaching their demise or should be discontinued. There exists a global phenomenon whereby Bitcoin and alternative cryptocurrencies are perceived as a means to promote greater openness and inclusivity in an outdated monetary system that currently favors a privileged few while disadvantaging the majority.

This leads us to the primary vulnerability of BTC, which is the absence of prevailing notions indicating its potential termination or shutdown in the foreseeable future. Nevertheless, it remains a risk and it is imperative that you regard it as such.

The key peril, in all its manifestations, lies in the potential eradication of BTC's ability to sustain its existence. The aforementioned risk is the primary concern, and the respective risks that arise from it serve to pinpoint the areas that may warrant concern.

There exists the possibility that governments may collectively opt to close it down due to concerns that its existence may undermine their sovereign authority. This assertion, despite being presented in various manners, is inherently motivated by self-interest. This viewpoint is posited by individuals who may lack comprehension of the fact that the emergence and eventual ubiquity of cryptocurrencies will primarily affect the viability of major financial institutions, resulting in their obsolescence. This is due to their proximity to the governing bodies, which results in a shared outlook on cryptocurrencies. They made multiple attempts at implementing BTC, but were unsuccessful on several occasions. The primary factor behind this is that the public exhibited resolute and unwavering support in significant numbers. Furthermore, there lacked a viable means to effectively enforce any potential prohibition on it, unless the internet were to be subjected to comprehensive censorship and control. Given that I am unable to envision such an occurrence occurring in the near future, it is difficult to establish the validity of this argument proclaiming the demise of BTC.

The subsequent risk that necessitates your consideration pertains to the capacity of an adequate number of nodes to effectively monitor the currency. We regard BTC and the blockchain as the central pillar of the system, serving as the authoritative ledger and comprehensive repository of the transactions executed. When one is able to effectively trace and link each individual block, the current state of the currency coin assumes an air of legitimacy. The entirety of the blockchain confers validity upon the cryptocurrency, and without it, its value has diminished significantly. The government of the present day confers legitimacy upon the fiat, yet it remains susceptible to shifting political inclinations and caprices. Trust is likewise a topic open to negotiation within the realm of fiat currencies. However, this is not the case with cryptocurrencies. The authenticity of these coins arises from an enduring, inflexible documentation of their existence and involvement in each transaction.

However, an issue arises from this situation, namely that the transaction rates, particularly in the presence of heightened trading activities, are causing the blockchain to expand at a rate close to 20 gigabytes per year. And it is anticipated that there will be a rise in this regard. In the event that each node assumes the responsibility of maintaining a comprehensive record of every transaction, it is anticipated that within a limited timeframe, there will be a scarcity of individuals or entities willing to accommodate the entirety of the ledger. Currently, the majority of existing nodes are lightweight, solely capturing transactions pertaining to their own wallet and transaction history. If the ledger file grows to an extensive size to the point where only a limited number of individuals diligently oversee its upkeep, it begins to pave the way for potential manipulation, if executed with expertise.

This poses a significant risk, and the accounting measures have yet to fully incorporate this factor. One potential concern that should be anticipated within the upcoming five-year period is the issue arising from the increasing size of the ledger. The employment of lite nodes helped to mitigate this risk, yet it remains a potential concern moving forward.

The following matter concerns the unauthorized infiltration of the system. In the blockchain system, a consensus mechanism known as the "majority consensus protocol" is employed. As per this protocol, when more than half (51%) of the distributed ledgers on all nodes collectively agree on the validity of a specific transaction, it is duly accepted and subsequently recorded across all the ledgers. Upon the occurrence of a valid transaction, the attainment of the 51% threshold occurs expeditiously, in fact reaching a percentage as high as 90%. The underlying cause for the inability to reach a 100% is the occasional offline status of certain nodes, resulting in their inability to record and verify transactions from their respective positions. Nevertheless, in the event that an individual were to invest considerable time and resources into subverting a majority (51%) of the network's nodes, it would invariably undermine the overall security and core functionality of Bitcoin (BTC) or any other cryptocurrency. Currently, the probability of that occurrence is quite slim, as the wallets and blockchain source codes undergo thorough peer review and are made publicly available as open source. Consequently, nothing is permitted on the blockchain unless it has undergone the process of verification and obtaining consensus. The system exhibits high levels of efficiency and enjoys global reach, thereby minimizing the associated risks to a considerable extent.

These risks encompass the majority of the potential threats Bitcoin (BTC) may face, which could significantly detriment the profitability of any open long positions held by traders. However, it is important to observe that the disadvantage is minimal. Here is why. With the exception of a coordinated government shutdown, if any of these events were to occur, the impact on the price would manifest gradually. It would not experience immediate worthlessness, but rather commence a gradual devaluation. Under such circumstances, you have two options available to you. There are two possible courses of action available to you: either engage in short selling of the coin or opt to liquidate your long position while incurring only minimal losses.

Please be advised of the following information that you must bear in mind. There have been numerous instances in which critics have pronounced the demise of the coin. Why? Due to unauthorized access or theft perpetrated by an individual. However, what they failed to observe was that regardless of the decrease in price resulting from the hack or theft, the potential losses were minimal and the recovery occurred within a short span of one or two days. Therefore, the potential negative impact of these risks is not significant, but presents two trading prospects—a position to sell on the occurrence of the event and a position to buy on the subsequent recovery. Numerous investors fail to recognize the significance of short positions and consequently overlook the opportunity to generate additional cash and gain profits. It is advisable to acquaint yourself with shorts, as this will enable you to successfully navigate and capitalize on both storms and surges when they arise. Additionally, they enhance your adaptability. The majority of individuals express dissatisfaction and frustration during unfavorable market conditions. In the event of a declining price, if you can devise an effective short position, you would stand to benefit from market movement in either direction, thus leading to contentment.

Now, let us redirect our attention to the potential vulnerabilities associated with the blockchain.

The predominant risk, with the exception of the plausible scenario of government intervention, a possibility that cannot be completely overlooked, lies in the fact that it is discernible in advance and can be mitigated by the community. To be precise, it presents itself as a valuable trading prospect.

Now, regarding the governmental restriction. If such a circumstance were to occur, the factor enabling BTC's progress would be the inherent inability to dismantle a peer-to-peer (P2P) system. An entity that is disaggregated and based on open-source principles cannot be completely eradicated. As the government intensifies its regulatory measures, it concurrently erodes its capacity to oversee and levy taxes on the subject matter. Ultimately, governments will come to realize, much like the majority have at present, that it is imperative to champion the technology rather than oppose it.

The risk that we have discussed here is both in terms of the individual currencies and to the blockchain in general. In a general sense, the blockchain refers to the notion of distributed record-keeping and updating of ledgers, a process that occurs uniformly across all nodes. It represents a shared characteristic across all cryptocurrencies, and any marginal or inconsequential alterations from one iteration of a cryptocurrency, for example, transitioning from BTC to Ethereum, can be considered superficial in nature. It is unlikely to bring about a radical transformation to the developed blockchain framework.

The risk that arises among different currencies is inherently relative. The potential vulnerability of a recently introduced cryptocurrency is greater when compared to that of a well-established one, considering that the level of adoption tends to correspond with its duration of existence. The level of risk associated with Bitcoin is negligible compared to a newly minted currency, for instance.

Mining With Cryptocurrency

Cryptocurrency mining involves the utilization of computational power to authenticate transactions through intricate cryptographic problem-solving, resulting in the creation of new digital coins upon successful verification. The verified transactions are promptly recorded on the publicly accessible distributed ledger and subsequently disseminated to all participants within the cryptocurrency network. The procedure of mining is intricately complex and necessitates the expertise of dedicated individuals referred to as "miners" to carry out this undertaking.

These intricate cryptographic calculations necessitate the use of specialized mining equipment, and those miners who successfully solve them shall receive compensation for their endeavors in the form of newly minted cryptocurrency coins, as well as an additional transaction fee (which varies based on the particular cryptocurrency mining procedure). Not all cryptocurrencies possess the capacity for mining akin to Bitcoin; certain coins are pre-mined and do not necessitate any form of mining procedure.

Miners engage in a competitive endeavor to outperform their peers and secure their position as the frontrunners in successfully addressing intricate cryptographic challenges. In the beginning, upon the introduction of Bitcoin, miners were initially rewarded with 50 coins upon successfully completing the mining process. Subsequently, this amount was reduced by half to 25 coins in 2014, and has since been further halved. Presently, the process of "Bitcoin mining" can yield a reward of 12.5 BTC for the successful verification of a transaction block.

In order to engage in cryptocurrency mining, it will be necessary to allocate a substantial amount of funds towards acquiring specialized hardware and associated software. This includes investing in an ASIC mining rig, procuring a comprehensive mining software package, obtaining membership to an online mining pool, subscribing to an online cryptocurrency exchange, and establishing a coin wallet.

It is imperative to allocate a dedicated well-ventilated space or chamber, equipped with adequate air conditioning, to accommodate the mining equipment due to the substantial heat it will generate during operation.

Cryptocurrency Mining strategies

Mining is regarded as a viable and sustainable investment approach for generating profits through cryptocurrency. In the early stages of Bitcoin's introduction, it was feasible to engage in mining using a personal computer equipped with a high-performance graphics processing unit (GPU). As the demand for this opportunity increased, a corresponding rise in competition ensued, resulting in heightened mining difficulty. Specially engineered mining equipment, known as the ASIC mining rig, has been specifically designed to excel in the task of efficiently mining cryptocurrencies, delivering heightened speed and effectiveness.

If one opts to pursue profit through Bitcoin mining, it is imperative to be prepared to undertake the additional endeavor of investing in the requisite hardware configuration, as well as devoting considerable time and energy. One possible alternative in a formal tone could be: "To commence mining on a smaller scale initially, a potential avenue is to consider acquiring a mining pool. This allows for the relatively diminished complexity of solving algorithms, since a shared transaction block will be distributed among numerous miners within the community." Cloud mining also has the potential to yield higher returns with minimal investment; however, it is prudent to remain wary of unscrupulous individuals seeking to deceive or defraud. Conduct thorough research and select a reputable 'cloud mining company.'

A range of mining approaches encompasses:

GPU Mining

One could argue that the resurgence of GPU mining in the market can be attributed to the increase in Bitcoin's mining difficulty. Due to the elevated mining difficulty associated with Bitcoin, the level of intricacy involved in solving the hash has increased. This discovery has presented a novel approach for miners to engage in 'mining alternative cryptocurrencies', wherein the computational demands for solving the algorithm are considerably less arduous in comparison to Bitcoin. Given the straightforward nature of the mining process, a miner can begin by utilizing a desktop equipped with a high-quality GPU card. Alternative cryptocurrencies such as Dash, Ether, and ZCash have proven to be lucrative for miners, particularly when their market capitalization surged to several hundred dollars.

Home Mining

If you are prepared to allocate a substantial monetary investment towards acquiring commendable hardware mining equipment, the process of establishing a mining operation within the confines of your residence should not present an overly challenging endeavor. To successfully engage in cryptocurrency mining, a set of essential requirements include possessing a functional computer, an ASIC mining rig, high-speed computing capabilities, specialized mining software, membership in a mining pool, adequate ventilation for temperature control, and access to a sufficient power supply.

Cloud Mining

If you wish to avoid investing monetary resources in logistics and maintenance for your hardware mining configuration, considering 'cloud mining' as a viable alternative is advisable. While cloud mining may result in a lower profit margin, it enables the generation of additional income to cover incidental expenses.

What is the most effective approach to leverage the optimal mining strategy?

Once you have made a selection regarding the cryptocurrency you intend to "mine," it will be necessary for you to attend to the following:

- Select the mining equipment
- Prepare the coin wallet
- Choose the mining pool
- Acquire the mining software ● Procure the mining application ● Attain the mining software ● Secure the mining program
- Commence

Select the mining apparatus

There is a plethora of cryptocurrency mining rigs readily accessible in the market. You may select the most suitable option by evaluating the cryptocurrency you intend to mine, considering the projected profitability, determining your financial capacity for investment, and taking into account the amount of time available for engagement in the endeavor. The consensus suggests that the Antminer S9 is the most cutting-edge and formidable mining device currently available.

Prepare the coin wallet" "Get the coin wallet prepared" "Ensure the coin wallet is ready" "Make sure the coin wallet is prepared" "Have the coin wallet ready

It is imperative to obtain a coin wallet in order to securely store the rewards (crypto coins) that you will accrue throughout the mining process. Digital wallets (already accessible through the corresponding exchanges), physical wallets on paper, wallets that are not connected to the internet (hardware wallets), and so forth. can be used. After successfully selecting an appropriate wallet, it is necessary to acquire the wallet address in order to transfer the acquired cryptocurrency from the exchange platform to your personal wallet. The wallet address consists of a lengthy combination of numerical and alphabetical characters. Please remember to create a backup of the .dat file, which is a copy of your wallet. This proves instrumental in mitigating incidents such as coin pilferage, data corruption, system failures, and similar scenarios.

Choose the mining collective.

The mining pool will be advantageous, as it allows a collective group of miners to consolidate their computational capabilities to enhance coin generation. Due to the increased participation of miners, the algorithm will be simplified, resulting in a reduced level of complexity in solving transaction blocks. Once the transaction blocks have been successfully solved, the cryptocurrency coins will be divided among the miners who have achieved success in solving the respective transaction block. Due to the accelerated mining process, the returns exhibit a consistent upward trend.

"Prior to selecting the mining pool, it is advisable to be cognizant of the following aspects:

- The methodology used to determine the calculation of rewards - The procedure through which rewards are computed - The mechanism employed to ascertain the calculation of rewards - The method by which rewards are assessed and quantified

- Fees associated with withdrawing funds

- The minimum and maximum charge for mining expenses.

- The rate at which the blocks are unveiled

- The procedure for withdrawing funds.

- The stability of the mining pool

Acquire the mining software.

Upon your selection of the mining rig, the mining program can be acquired. There is a limited number of mining rigs that possess their own mining software.

Bitminer is an example. The Macminer mining software is compatible with Apple computers, while the 50Miner software is designed for utilization on Windows-based systems.

Get started

Has your mining infrastructure been prepared? Certainly! Begin the process by accessing the mining website through the input of your designated username and corresponding password.

Allow us to commence.

One could develop a cryptocurrency mining strategy as a means of initiating revenue generation through the utilization of virtual currency. If you are limited by a financial constraint and unable to allocate significant funds towards the acquisition of the necessary hardware for mining, you can commence operations on a smaller scale.

Procedures for engaging in the mining endeavor

Ensure that you acquire a high-performance graphics card and utilize a computer equipped with a top-tier processor as an initial step.

Over time, you may accumulate the funds obtained from mining in order to acquire a high-quality ASIC miner and sustain the operation. For those seeking to establish a more robust mining portfolio, it is advisable to diligently save the proceeds from mining activities and procure two additional ASIC miners to establish a comprehensive mining setup.

- One possible approach is to initiate the process of GPU mining for Bytecoin or Litecoin.

The mobile application offered by the cryptocurrency mining pool 'Minergate' enables users to engage in mining activities using their smartphones as well. It is not advisable to engage in mobile mining.

- From what I have observed, Minergate is an ideal choice for beginners seeking a user-friendly mining pool that facilitates mining with their own hardware configuration.

- If you want to mine Bitcoin, you can even use their Bitcoin cloud mining setup.

- EOBOT presents itself as an additional cloud mining platform that provides the opportunity to commence mining activities without any monetary investment (at no cost to the user).

Let us postulate that you have engaged in GPU mining using Minergate to extract a few Bytecoins. You have the option to transfer the Bytecoin to EOBOT and subsequently trade it for any other cryptocurrency listed on their dashboard, taking into consideration their respective price valuation.

The option 'Claim Free Coins' can be advantageous as it allows users to acquire 1 Dogecoin every fifteen minutes, with a withdrawal limit set at a mere 10.

EOBOT provides round-the-clock Scrypt contracts, five-year SHA256 contracts, and 24-hour SHA256 contracts that you can acquire through the exchange of your cryptocurrency coins.

These tools can prove beneficial in the process of Bitcoin mining, as they enable the conversion of the Bytecoin earned from GPU mining into SHA256 contracts.

- You are now able to utilize these SHA256 contracts for cloud mining Bitcoin, resulting in significant profit potential when compared to Bytecoins.

- The earned Bitcoins can subsequently be retained for long-term advantages through adherence to the 'buy and hold' approach.

Ultimately, the process entails mining a lesser-valued alternative cryptocurrency (specifically Bytecoin in this instance) and subsequently utilizing said cryptocurrency as an investment for cloud mining the renowned digital currency (Bitcoin), which in turn can be retained for long-term advantages.

CHAPTER SUMMARY:

This chapter provides an overview of the following:

- The process of extracting digital currencies through computational algorithms.

- Extractive methodology

The Advantages of Adhering to the Mining Strategy

"• Methods to initiate the process "• Approaches to commence the undertaking "• Strategies for commencing the endeavor "• Techniques for getting the ball rolling

Blockchain Applications and Perspectives

As previously indicated in the initial section of this chapter, the blockchain technology, propelled by the advent of Bitcoin, has discovered its primary and inaugural utility in the realm of transactions.

By means of the Distributed Ledger Transaction, it is indeed feasible for every transaction to be initiated and concluded directly between two individuals through the Internet, rendering the involvement of a centralized certifying authority unnecessary, as it takes on the responsibility of system trust and consent delegation. However, utilization in transactions is merely one of the potential applications encompassed within the vast array of functionalities provided by the blockchain.

In order to grasp the extensive range of applications of this technology, it is essential to consider the various scenarios wherein two distinct groups of entities are established: those who exert control and those who are subject to control.

The aforementioned categories pertain to a highly centralized system, wherein the dependability, credibility, and safeguarding of the system are entrusted to a higher authority embodied by the controllers.

Considering the fact that the blockchain, utilizing proof of work as an illustration, enables the establishment of a collective and transparent ledger accessible to all individuals, wherein trust and consensus are attained through a decentralized procedure, it becomes apparent how this system can, in numerous instances, supplant centralized systems by surmounting the division between those in control and those being controlled, in favor of a more democratic mechanism where each participant actively competes to attain trust and consensus within the system.

The potential for employing blockchain extends beyond the transaction sector, encompassing a wide array of potential application domains in which this technology is expected to have a significant transformative impact in the near future. (Figure 10)

Figure 10 - Possible Utilizations of the Blockchain technology

According to evaluations conducted by prominent experts in the blockchain industry, we now undertake an examination of the domains in which the eventual adoption of this technology is anticipated to yield significant effects.

Financial Sectors

Financial markets serve as a prime illustration of centralized systems in operation.

Indeed, there exist constant evaluations conducted by both public and private entities, with the purpose of verifying the validity of implemented actions. These evaluations serve the crucial role of providing assurance and instilling trust in the system. In these industries, blockchain technology can pose a substantial risk as it possesses the potential to eliminate traditional intermediaries and hence cause the obsolescence of numerous roles that have hitherto been deemed indispensable. One illustration of this phenomenon can be witnessed in the realm of banking, wherein the prominent position it holds in facilitating transactions and acting as an intermediary would erode if said transactions were to occur in a decentralized fashion via cryptocurrencies. However, it is imperative to acknowledge the significant benefits that the implementation of blockchain technology would bestow upon the financial industry in relation to operational efficacy, swiftness, and expenditure.

The Ripple Lab case, which revolves around the revolutionizing impact of their cryptocurrency on interbank exchanges and relationships, is a noteworthy topic that will be thoroughly scrutinized in the final chapter.

Furthermore, apart from the aforementioned example of NASDAQ Linq, which employs blockchain technology for stock and bond transactions, the banking and insurance industries can also benefit from this technology in establishing a digital identity for their clients. This would involve storing all relevant information in a register that is both immutable and accessible to all parties involved. This facilitates the evaluation of a risk profile, such as when extending a mortgage or establishing an insurance agreement.

One noteworthy example of the banking system's engagement in blockchain and cryptocurrencies is undeniably exemplified by Goldman Sachs18. Indeed, the world's leading investment bank has acquired Polinex, a longstanding Bitcoin exchange, through its subsidiary Circle, for a substantial sum of 400 million dollars. Polinex serves as a trading platform where users engage in the buying and selling of various cryptocurrencies such as BTC and Ethereum, as well as traditional currencies like dollars and euros. The primary goal of this investment is to establish a leading position within the cryptocurrency industry, as specified by the present investment director, who does, however, recognize cryptocurrencies as a speculative financial phenomenon.

The crowdfunding sector will also be subject to investment from the innovative influx of blockchain technology. Indeed, the essence of the revolution lies in the elimination of the central entity required to facilitate the crowdfunding campaign, such as Kickstarter, thereby enabling start-ups to attain independent funding similar to that seen in initial coin offerings (ICOs).

Smart Contract

There are numerous sectors that will be subject to regulation pertaining to the innovative concept of "digital and smart contracts." While the final chapter will encompass a discussion on smart contracts in relation to the Ethereum cryptocurrency, this section serves to provide a preliminary understanding of key concepts.

The term "smart contract" refers to a specific type of computer-based contract that is established and administered on a network. It is designed to automatically execute and take effect when certain pre-determined conditions, as outlined within its terms, are met. Notably, no manual input or intervention from the involved parties is required to activate the contract, thereby eliminating the potential for fraudulent activities.

A fundamental necessity intrinsic to conventional agreements is the establishment of mutual trust, whereby all participants faithfully uphold their respective responsibilities.

Conversely, smart contracts do not rely on the reliability of the counterparty's dedication; instead, they assure trust through their pre-programmed, computerized, and autonomous execution, eliminating the element of human discretion.

The computer codes governing the smart contracts on the blockchain platform function to ensure the indisputable execution of transactions. These smart contracts have the potential for application in various contexts beyond currency transactions, encompassing any circumstance involving the transfer of ownership.

Intelligent Assets and Digitized Entitlements

The blockchain can serve as a comprehensive repository, functioning as an inventory system, to meticulously monitor and document a wide array of transactions and information. It governs and accurately chronicles both corporeal possessions (e.g., currencies, real estate) and intangible assets like intellectual property.

Properties that are recorded in the blockchain ledger acquire the designation of smart properties, enabling their administration and transfer through the utilization of smart contracts.

When discussing the topic of rights, such as the copyright pertaining to music and books, it is possible to digitally record and authenticate them using a blockchain protocol. This enables individuals to assert their ownership over a specific right and facilitates the transfer of said right by means of relinquishing their associated private key. It is noteworthy in this particular framework to make reference to the acquisition of Mediachain by Spotify, a prominent player in the domain of digital music. This transaction has facilitated the establishment of a blockchain registry to enhance the transparency and effectiveness in the administration of royalty payments to musicians for their creative works.

An additional illustration of digital property management pertains to the financing of a vehicle acquisition, which can be exemplified by the straightforward scenario of entering into a financial lease.

It is plausible that the regulation could be facilitated through the implementation of a smart contract, wherein the transfer of ownership of the vehicle from the financing company to the financed party would be unconditionally contingent upon the full payment of the final installment as stipulated in the leasing contract.

An additional factor that could be taken into account regarding tangible assets pertains to real estate, a sector in which transactions are marked by substantial bureaucratic processes.

Indeed, the administration of notarial instruments and other records could be facilitated using a blockchain database, thereby enhancing the efficiency and openness of real estate transactions, and diminishing the financial burden of such transactions.

The collaborative database could thus serve as a land registry, encompassing the recording of property deeds, transactions, permits, and other documents typically overseen by public authorities, without the requirement of a certifying entity.

Digital Identity Management

Furthermore, within this particular framework, the successful deployment of a joint, unchangeable, and protected repository through the application of encryption would facilitate enhanced effectiveness in the realm of digital administration. This can be attributed to the susceptibility of centralized databases to cyber threats, which enable unauthorized access to the entirety of customer data stored within the system, including online identities.

Conversely, a blockchain-powered identification system employing cryptographic digital signatures would enable enhanced security and uncontested administration of digital identities. This technological application is under development by multiple corporate entities and governmental bodies, including the Estonian government. Its potential lies in expanding decentralized governance to encompass not only digital identities but also driver's licenses, passports, and birth and marriage certificates.

Digital Vote

Building upon the rationale employed to establish digital identities, employing a blockchain ledger facilitates seamless verification of an individual's identity for an assortment of online transactions, including digital voting.

The execution of the latter has encountered setbacks in numerous nations owing to concerns related to security and privacy. Denmark, Norway, and Estonia are among the nations that have endeavored to transition the conventional voting procedure into a digital format. However, only the latter has effectively executed expansive digital voting initiatives. By means of a voting mechanism based on blockchain technology, individuals who participate in the voting process would be granted the opportunity to verify the legitimacy of their vote, thereby upholding their right to anonymity and confidentiality. Furthermore, such a provision would serve to enhance the accessibility of voting to a considerably greater number of individuals, thereby potentially fostering heightened civic engagement in the political realm.

Sharing Economy

The sharing economy has gained considerable traction and pervasive influence in recent years. In the given context, consider ride-hailing platforms like Uber, as well as accommodations booking platforms like Airbnb. Nevertheless, in the most renowned platforms for sharing, there exists an intermediary in all instances of interactions and transactions.

By leveraging the utilization of blockchain technology, which aligns harmoniously with the principles of a collaborative economy, it becomes feasible to eradicate all intermediaries, thereby enabling the development of fully decentralized applications.

More specifically, the utilization of blockchain technology would ensure the integrity and authenticity of reviews, a crucial factor in the decision-making process for purchases, rendering them immutable.

Public Services (Utilities)

Furthermore, aside from the provision of public services, such as the management of digital identities or land registry, the utilization of blockchain applications could also be expanded to encompass utilities, specifically the distribution of energy. In forthcoming times, it is plausible that smart grid infrastructure could facilitate households in not only consuming energy according to their requirements but also trading surplus energy back to the power grid. This would foster the emergence of a supplementary market, where each user could engage in peer-to-peer transactions with fellow network members.

Health Sector

A blockchain is an extensively distributed database wherein modifications applied to one copy of the ledger are promptly reflected on all copies, thereby enabling all network participants to possess continuously updated data and information across each database replica. This functionality implies a prospective future implementation within the realm of healthcare.

It is necessary to mention that each patient who comes into contact with a new physician or medical facility must complete multiple documentation in order to establish their medical record, which is not distributed or shared across different healthcare institutions. The capacity to store patient records in a centralized repository would enable medical practitioners, healthcare institutions, and insurance providers to facilitate effective and expedited communication through the exchange of data.

Predictions and Gambling

Numerous emerging enterprises that specialize in blockchain technology are endeavoring to revolutionize the gambling industry, specifically in prediction markets, encompassing areas such as weather forecasting and financial market performance evaluation. Among the cryptocurrencies exhibiting significant growth, it is imperative to highlight the commendable progress of Augur. Augur's endeavors center around the creation of a prediction market, wherein every user stands to gain from the outcome of a given event. Therefore, Augur intends to establish a decentralized platform with the purpose of evaluating the likelihood of a particular event transpiring, thereby enabling its users to engage in the act of wagering.

Production Processes

Even within the realm of production processes, the possibility exists to re-engineer numerous operations, thereby enabling cost savings or enhancements in value. Supply chain is a key focal point when considering the most appealing manufacturing processes for the adoption of blockchain technology. In the context of a supply chain, the utilization of a distributed database would facilitate improved inventory management and enhance transparency throughout the entirety of the product lifecycle. This database would effectively and unalterably document the various stages of the product and ascertain the provenance of the goods.

Walmart, the prominent American retail corporation, presently employs blockchain technology for the purpose of monitoring and recording the transportation of pork products from Chinese farms to its various retail establishments.

Chapter 8 – The Negative Aspects of the Cryptocurrency Market

Engaging in asset trading can engender a profound sense of dependency. When seasoned traders observe the emergence of a trending asset class, it typically piques their interest. The majority of these serial traders are reluctant to forgo any potential opportunities. Their sense of self-importance and their financial status rely on making decisions that yield profit.

Previously, it was the stock market that commanded the focus of these avid traders. Over time, the speculative aspect of the Foreign Exchange Trade captured the majority of their focus. At present, bitcoin and other cryptocurrencies have emerged as the most recent financial assets within the market.

The substantial surge in market participants led to a notable surge in the value of cryptocurrencies over the course of last year. A considerable number of these traders refrain from entering the market, driven by the anticipation of price appreciation. A significant proportion of individuals possess strategies aimed at influencing prices. In the initial month of 2017, during the nascent stages of bitcoin's price surge, global governments had not yet expressed apprehension towards the cryptocurrency. As a result, there was a dearth of regulatory measures in place pertaining to the transactional activities involved in the buying and selling of cryptocurrency. In the absence of regulatory frameworks, the unregulated trade attracted the interest of numerous individuals with nefarious intentions.

Fake ICOs

In 2017, there were countless illegal schemes surrounding the different cryptocurrencies. The establishment of counterfeit initial coin offering (ICO) platforms emerged as a frequent fraudulent tactic. Telemarketers reached out to numerous prospective investors, extending invitations to invest in novel cryptocurrencies with the promise of doubling their value within a year. It was widely observed that such an outcome was not deemed implausible within the context of bitcoin and Ethereum. Consequently, numerous individuals inadvertently succumbed to such deceptions.

Both investors and users of cryptocurrency should ensure their involvement is limited to the most widely recognized cryptocurrencies as a starting point. Refrain from pursuing investments in nascent ICOs at this point in time. These individuals engaging in fraudulent activities possess a high level of proficiency and expertise in their craft. They will establish a compelling façade in order to persuade both you and others that their initial coin offerings (ICOs) possess genuine credibility. It is possible that they possess an online platform containing comprehensive details regarding their purported currency. Nevertheless, ultimately, all these validation tools prove to be mere illusions.

It is imperative to ensure that you consult reliable financial sources such as Investopedia or Yahoo Finance prior to divulging your financial information to initial coin offerings. By exercising thorough research and investigation, you will be capable of circumventing fraudulent schemes such as these.

Credit Card Scams

In numerous instances over the last year, individuals have succumbed to a deception that would prove ineffective in actuality. This plan unfolds as follows. An individual or a collective endeavor to masquerade as credible enterprises on the internet, seeking to acquire bitcoin or other widely-used cryptocurrencies.

They will come across receptive purchasers who are eager to divest a portion of their bitcoin holdings. These fraudulent individuals possess various tactics to create an appearance of plausibility in their actions. Rather than purchasing the entire amount of bitcoin, for instance, they will inquire whether it is possible to acquire only half due to their current financial constraints. Alternatively, they might propose exchanging it for an alternative form of cryptocurrency prior to confirming their intention to provide payment in cash.

They undertake these actions with the intention of persuading you that they are bona fide purchasers who simply lack expertise in handling cryptocurrencies. Ultimately, they will reach a consensus regarding the transaction and furnish you with a credit card number accompanied by a valid pin for verification purposes. Believing that the transaction has been finalized, you or any other party seeking to derive financial gain from one's digital currencies proceeds to transfer the said currency to the intended recipient. Following a period of approximately one week, the transaction made with the credit card is alerted for scrutiny. The bank transaction has been invalidated due to the report of credit card theft. The information furnished by the purchaser is inaccurate. While the authentic credit card holder receives reimbursement for their funds, you, on the contrary, lack the capability to retrieve your cryptocurrency. That is just the nature of a cryptocurrency. The identity remains undisclosed and cannot be undone unless there is mutual consent from both parties involved.

In the absence of an identifiable individual, no formal proceedings can be initiated as the perpetrator's identity remains elusive.

Manipulative Trading Schemes

In addition to the aforementioned illicit strategies, the practice of artificially inflating and subsequently divesting from stocks, known as pumping and dumping, is frequently observed within the realm of cryptocurrency trading. If one is not well-acquainted with this scheme, it typically commences with either a counterfeit ICO or even a genuine one. The crucial aspect lies in its affordability, ensuring accessibility for a wide range of individuals.

Following the selection of the ICO, the organized crime syndicate consolidates their funds to allocate them exclusively towards their desired currency. After injecting a substantial amount of liquidity into the currency, its valuation commences an upward trajectory. Subsequently, the group proceeds to implement the second phase of the strategy, wherein the telemarketers they have on their payroll are instructed to take action. These telemarketers market the cryptocurrency with claims suggesting it has potential to rival bitcoin. They swiftly and efficiently engage in sales, transitioning seamlessly from one interaction to the next until they achieve the desired purchase. They make grandiose pledges to the individual they are contacting, compelling them to invest their utmost financial resources in the market.

Once the currency has attained its zenith value, the individuals affiliated with the organized crime syndicate commence withdrawing their personal funds from the system. Subsequently, they proceed to reap the financial gains, leaving behind all the individuals they deceived into purchasing the currency.

As they are divesting their funds from the market, they continue to maintain an active team of telemarketers, assuring their investors to remain invested as the downturn is merely transitory. This will guarantee that the individuals comprising the criminal organization have sufficient duration to dispose of their respective assets. At present, the individuals remaining in the market at a later stage are susceptible to incurring substantial financial losses.

Money Laundering

Not every criminal activity witnessed within the cryptocurrency market results in individuals being victimized. Occasionally, this market serves as a means for unscrupulous individuals to legitimize their illicit funds. Cash obtained through illicit means poses challenges when it comes to its expenditure. Should the government observe an individual who lacks a disclosed profession engaging in extravagant expenditures amounting to millions of dollars, suspicions are likely to arise.

In order to evade legal scrutiny, felons must exhibit ingenuity in their tactics for relocating their funds. Previously, they were compelled to collaborate with unscrupulous bankers, lawyers, and even politicians for the purpose of transferring their funds and granting them legal status.

Presently, though, they have employed an alternative approach to discreetly transferring their funds using cryptocurrency, thereby evading government detection. Prior to attaining popularity as an investment asset, cryptocurrency had already established itself as a well-adopted means of transaction within the realms of criminal activities. Websites within the depths of the dark web universally embrace cryptocurrencies as a means to preserve the anonymity of their users' identities.

www.ingramcontent.com/pod-product-compliance
Lightning Source LLC
Chambersburg PA
CBHW050245120526
44590CB00016B/2224